Wild guinea pigs like to live in big family groups. It is unkind to keep just one guinea pig as a pet.

GUINEA PIG FACT

Guinea pigs were first brought to Britain about 250 years ago.

3

The guinea pig for you

There are many kinds of guinea pigs. They have different coloured fur and different fur lengths. Some, like the sheltie or Peruvian guinea pig, are long-haired.

short-haired guinea pig

GUINEA PIGS

MICHAELA MILLER

Contents

Words in bold, like this, are explained in the glossary on page 23.

Wild ones

Wild guinea pigs are called cavies and most of them live in Peru. They like to spend their days eating grass, leaves and plant stems. They sleep and shelter under logs and in caves and **burrows**.

wild guinea pigs

GUINEA PIG FACT

Guinea pigs can live for up to seven years.

Long-haired guinea pigs are quite difficult to look after. Their coats need a lot of brushing to keep them tangle-free. Short-haired guinea pigs are best for first-time owners.

5

Where to find your guinea pig

Animal shelters are often looking for good homes for guinea pigs. You can also buy your guinea pigs from **breeders**. A good breeder will let you ask lots of questions. They will check their guinea pigs are going to good homes.

A vet could let you know about local breeders and animal shelters. Do not buy your guinea pig from anywhere that looks dirty.

 GUINEA PIG FACT

Guinea pigs need to be kept warm in the winter.

Healthy guinea pigs

Choose two male guinea pigs or two females from the same **litter**. They should be between six and eleven weeks old. They should have smooth coats and clean ears, eyes, mouths, noses and tails. Healthy guinea pigs run around their home quite happily.

young guinea pigs eating lettuce

GUINEA PIG FACT

If you put two male or two female adult guinea pigs together who don't know each other, they may fight.

Do not choose a guinea pig that seems to have no energy and is crouching in a corner. It is probably not very well.

Safe hands

Move towards your guinea pig from the front rather than from the side. This does not frighten it so much. Pick it up very gently with one hand under its bottom and the other around its shoulders.

Do not let it wriggle or jump from your arms because it could really hurt itself.

Your guinea pigs will probably like being brushed gently with a baby's hairbrush every day.

Guinea pigs can be very timid and can get upset if you hold them a lot.

Feeding time

Guinea pigs need lots of water. Attach a drip-fed water bottle with a metal spout to the side of your guinea pigs' house and exercise area, and make sure it is always full.

GUINEA PIG FACT

Guinea pigs need lots of vitamin C, which they get from greens and vegetables.

You can buy special guinea pig food from pet shops. Feed each guinea pig about 50-80 grams every day and a 100 grams mixture of dandelion leaves, grass and raw vegetables. Put the food in heavy bowls.

Home sweet home

Get the biggest house you can for your guinea pigs. For two guinea pigs it should be at least 120 x 60 x 45 cm. It should have a sleeping area with a solid door and a living area with a mesh front. You should also give them a **run** in the garden when the weather is good.

house

run

The house should be high off the ground. In cold weather it should be moved inside into a garage or the house.

an indoor exercise area

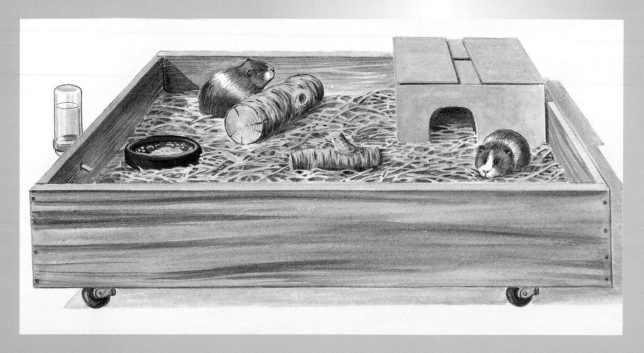

GUINEA PIG FACT

In the winter guinea pigs will also need an indoor exercise area.

Keeping clean

The guinea pigs' house should be cleaned out every day to keep your pets healthy. Wet patches and droppings should always be removed.

GUINEA PIG FACT

The house will need to be thoroughly cleaned at least four times a year.

Guinea pigs need deep, soft bedding like hay and straw to sleep and **burrow** in. Under this, and throughout the whole house, there should be a five-cm-deep layer of **peat**, cat **litter** or wood chippings.

At the vet's

Take your guinea pigs to the vet once a year for a check-up. The vet will look out for things like overlong teeth and claws.

Watch your guinea pigs every day very carefully for signs of illness. Always check their teeth, eyes, nose and bottom. If they do not want to eat, seem tired or even seem to have a cold, take them to the vet immediately.

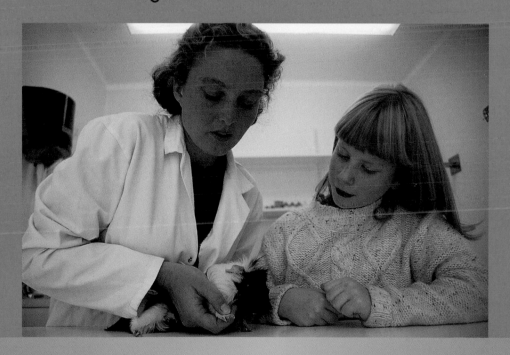

GUINEA PIG FACT

A hardwood **gnawing block** will give your guinea pig something to gnaw on and stop its teeth getting too long.

No more babies

It really is not a good idea to let your guinea pigs have babies. Female guinea pigs (sows) can have five litters a year and four babies in each **litter**.

GUINEA PIG FACT

If rabbits and guinea pigs meet when they are very young they can live together. Each should have its own private space in their house.

Finding homes for the babies can be a real problem. It is quite difficult to get guinea pigs **neutered** so they do not have babies. So always keep guinea pigs of the same sex together.

A note from the RSPCA

Pets are lots of fun and can end up being our best friends. These animal friends need very special treatment – plenty of kindness, a good home, the right food and lots of attention.

This book helps you to understand what your pet needs. It also shows you how you can play an important part in looking after your pet. But the adults in your family must be in overall charge of any family pet. This means that they should get advice from a vet and read about how to give your pet the best care.

Why not become a member of the RSPCA's Animal Action Club. You'll receive a membership card, badge, stickers and magazine. To find out how to join, write to RSPCA Animal Action Club, Causeway, Horsham, West Sussex RH12 1HG.

 # FURTHER READING

Glossary

animal shelters   also known as centres or homes. There are lots of these shelters all around the country which look after unwanted pets and try to find them new homes. The RSPCA has about 50 animal centres in England and Wales.

breeders   people who let their guinea pigs have babies. They then sell the babies.

burrows   underground holes and tunnels

gnawing block   a bark-covered log of wood for guinea pigs to chew on. This stops their teeth from getting too long.

litter   a group of new born guinea pigs

neutered   an operation which stops an animal from having babies

peat   soil used to line the bottom of the guinea pigs' house

run   an outdoor area where the guinea pigs can run free when the weather is good. It should be fenced on all sides with a mesh cover on the top. This keeps the guinea pigs safe from cats, dogs and birds.

Index

First published in Great Britain by Heinemann Library, Halley Court, Jordan Hill, Oxford OX2 8EJ, a division of Reed Educational and Professional Publishing Ltd
OXFORD FLORENCE PRAGUE MADRID ATHENS MELBOURNE AUCKLAND KUALA LUMPUR SINGAPORE TOKYO IBADAN NAIROBI KAMPALA
JOHANNESBURG GABORONE PORTSMOUTH NH CHICAGO MEXICO CITY SAO PAULO
© RSPCA 1997
The moral right of the proprietor has been asserted.

Designed by Nicki Wise and Lisa Nutt
Illustrations by Michael Strand
Colour reproduction by Colourpath, London
Printed in Hong Kong / China

02
10 9 8 7 6 5 4
ISBN 0 431 03373 0
This title is also available in hardback edition.

British Library Cataloguing in Publication Data
Miller, Michaela
Guinea Pigs. - (Pets)
1.Guinea Pigs - Juvenile literature
I .Title II . Royal Society for the Prevention of Cruelty to Animals
636.9'3234

Acknowledgements
The Publishers would like to thank the following for permission to reproduce photographs:
Dave Bradford pp4, 5, 7, 10-13, 20, 21; Bruce Coleman Ltd/ p2 Gunter Zeisler; NHPA/ p3 E A Janes; RSPCA/ pp6 Colin Seddon , 8 Angela Hampton, 9 Judyth Platt, 18, 19 Tim Sambrook.
Cover photographs reproduced with permission of: RSPCA
Our thanks to Ann Head and her pets; Pippa Bush, Bill Swan and Jim Philips for their help in the preparation of this book; Pets Mart for the kind loan of equipment; the children of Oaklands Infants School.
Every effort has been made to contact copyright holders of any material reproduced in this book. Any omissions will be rectified in subsequent printings if notice is given to the Publisher.